KINGFISHER
READERS

level

2

In the
Rainforest

Claire Llewellyn and
Thea Feldman

KINGFISHER

NEW YORK

KINGFISHER
LONDON & NEW YORK

Copyright © Kingfisher 2014
Published in the United States by Kingfisher,
175 Fifth Ave., New York, NY 10010
Kingfisher is an imprint of Macmillan Children's Books, London.
All rights reserved.

Distributed in the U.S. and Canada by Macmillan,
175 Fifth Ave., New York, NY 10010

Library of Congress Cataloging-in-Publication data has been applied for.

Series editor: Thea Feldman
Literacy consultant: Ellie Costa, Bank Street College, New York

ISBN: 978-0-7534-7144-9 (HB)
ISBN: 978-0-7534-7145-6 (PB)

Kingfisher books are available for special promotions and
premiums. For details contact: Special Markets Department,
Macmillan, 175 Fifth Ave., New York, NY 10010.

For more information, please visit
www.kingfisherbooks.com

Printed in China
9 8 7 6 5 4 3 2 1
1TR/0913/WKT/UG/105MA

Picture credits
The Publisher would like to thank the following for permission to reproduce their material.
Every care has been taken to trace copyright holders. However, if there have been unintentional
omissions or failure to trace copyright holders, we apologize and will, if informed, endeavor
to make corrections in any future edition.

Top = t; Bottom = b; Center = c; Left = l; Right = r
Cover Shutterstock/Dr. Morley Read; FLPA/Konrad Wothe/Minden Pictures; Pages 4 Shutterstock/tandemich;
5t Shutterstock/kkaplin; 5b Frank Lane Picture Agency (FLPA)/Minden Pictures/Mark Jones; 6 Shutterstock/
Dhoxax; 7t FLPA/Minden Pictures/ Murray Cooper; 7b FLPA/Minden Pictures/Pete Oxford; 8 FLPA/Minden
Pictures/Pete Oxford; 9t Shutterstock/Steve Bower; 9b FLPA/Minden Pictures /Michael & Patricia Fogden;
10 FLPA/Minden Pictures /Michael & Patricia Fogden; 11 KF Archive; 12 FLPA/Imagebroker/Konrad Wothe;
13t FLPA/Minden Pictures /Michael & Patricia Fogden; 13b Getty/Tim Laman; 14 Alamy/Caro; 15 FLPA/
Peter Davey; 16 FLPA/Minden Pictures /Michael & Patricia Fogden; 17 Alamy/blickwinkel; 18 Shutterstock/
Aleksandar Todorovic; 19 Shutterstock/Brandon Alms; 20 Shutterstock/Antonio Clemens; 21t Shutterstock/
Cathy Keifer; 21b FLPA/Minden Pictures/Pete Oxford; 22–23 KF Archive; 24 FLPA/Photo Researchers;
25t Alamy/John Warburton-Lee Photography; 25b Alamy/Octavio Campos Salles; 26t naturepl.com/Visuals
Unlimited; 26–27 Shutterstock/Frontpage; 27t naturepl.com/Nick Gordon; 28–29 Shutterstock/Stephane
Bidouze; 28 FLPA/Minden Pictures/Konrad Wothe; 29 FLPA/ImageBroker; 30–31 KF Archive;
30t naturepl.com/Doug Wechsler.

Contents

A hot, rainy place   4

Rainforest plants   6

Plants provide food   8

Life at every layer   10

Some plant eaters   12

Some meat eaters   14

Speaking up   16

Bright colors   18

Blending in   20

Rainforest rivers   22

Village life   24

Vanishing places   26

Important places   28

Saving rainforests   30

Glossary   32

A hot, rainy place

A rainforest is a forest where it rains a lot, and temperatures are about 80°F (27°C).

Rainforests are found near the **equator**.

They each have many plants and animals that live nowhere else in the world.

Rainforest plants

Plants grow well in a warm, wet, and sunny place.

They grow all year long in a rainforest.

Trees are
the world's
tallest plants.

Some trees in
rainforests
can be 200 feet
(61 meters) tall.

Plants provide food

Rainforest plants provide food
for many animals.

The animals eat the stems, leaves,
flowers, and fruit of the plants.

Animals also find shelter
in rainforest plants.

Life at every layer

Trees and other plants grow at their own special height in a rainforest. This is called a layer.

Animals are at every level or layer.

Some live high up in the **canopy**.

Big animals, like the jaguar, live on the ground.

Some plant eaters

Leaf-cutter ants live in rainforests in South America.

They chop leaves with their strong jaws.

Hummingbirds eat **nectar** from flowers in a rainforest canopy.

Monkeys eat fruit that grows on tree branches.

Some meat eaters

Some animals in a rainforest
eat other animals.

They are called meat eaters
or predators.

Eagles in the canopy
catch monkeys or **sloths**
in their sharp claws.

Tarantulas on the ground
grab insects, frogs, or mice
with their long fangs.

Speaking up

Rainforests are so leafy that
it can be hard for some animals
to see each other.

So they make noise!
Frogs croak, birds squawk,
and monkeys howl.

Animals also call out to warn
each other about dangers.

Bright colors

Some animals have bright colors that are easy to see in a green forest.

Birds like these can find mates because of their bright colors.

Brightly colored rainforest frogs
have dangerous **poisons** in them.

Their colors warn predators
not to eat them.

Blending in

Some animals are hard to find because their colors or shapes help them blend into the forest.

This stick insect and lizard use **camouflage** to hide from predators.

Some predators, like the ocelot,
blend into the forest too,
so they can sneak up on their **prey**.

Rainforest rivers

Rain puts even more water into rainforest streams and rivers.

Many animals live in rainforest rivers.

Long snakes called anacondas,
small alligators called caimans,
and fish with sharp teeth
called piranhas all live in
rainforest rivers in South America.

Village life

People have lived in rainforests for thousands of years.

Today they live in villages, in houses made of wood and leaves.

They know which plants are good to eat, and which can be used to help heal sicknesses.

They know how to hunt and fish too.

25

Vanishing places

Rainforests around the world are being destroyed.

Trees are being chopped down and sold as lumber.

The land is also being cleared
so roads and farms can be built.

In some cleared rainforests,
people dig **mines** in the ground.

Important places

Rainforests are important for our planet.

They provide places for thousands of plants and animals to live.